G000155484

Excuses and Lies
Lines for All Occasions

KNOCK KNOCK

LOS ANGELES, CALIFORNIA

Created and published by Knock Knock
11111 Jefferson Blvd. #5167
Culver City, CA 90231
knockknockstuff.com

This book is a work of humor meant solely for entertainment purposes.
Actually utilizing the lines contained herein may be illegal or lead to
bodily injury. The publisher and anyone associated with the production
of this book do not advocate breaking the law. In no event will Knock
Knock be liable to any reader for any damages, including direct, indi-
rect, incidental, special, consequential, or punitive arising out of or in
connection with the use of the lines contained in this book. So there.

ISBN: 978-1-68349-261-0
UPC: 825703-50125-4

20 19 18 17 16 15 14 13 12 11 10 9 8 7 6 5 4 3 2 1

Contents

INTRO —————————————— 7
Preparing to deliver effective deception

THE WORKPLACE ——————————— 11
When you just can't manage it

LIKED ONES ———————————— 25
When the truth will hurt

LOVED ONES ———————————— 39
When they just don't get it

SELF-DECEPTIONS ————————— 53
When it's so not your fault

ADULTING ————————————— 67
When real life demands dishonesty

FAMOUSLY INFAMOUS ——————— 81
When the stakes are high

Intro

Preparing to Deliver Effective Deception

Excuses and lies are a necessary part of life. Six-month-olds begin their careers as proud fibbers with fake laughter and cries, and it's all downhill from there. In fact, if anyone says they don't lie, they're lying. Scientists have demonstrated that excuses and lies paved our evolutionary path by allowing us simultaneously to advance our own interests and to cement our role within our group.

Would we ever get our dream job if we said we couldn't type? Could we maintain our clique status if we said "I hate your new haircut?" Successful lying promotes survival of the fittest—the fittest, of course, are the liars.

When it comes to saving friendships, dignity, or our own skins, honesty is, quite simply, overrated. Being truthful can ruin marriages, sabotage negotiations, and possibly bring an end to the world as we know it. In his essay "On the Decay of the Art of Lying," no lesser light than Mark Twain acknowledged, "Everybody lies—every day; every hour; awake; asleep; in his dreams; in his joy; in his mourning." The question is not whether to lie or tell the truth—the question is how to lie well.

While all of us are liars, not everybody experiences the easy flow of words to lips, and that's where this book comes in. In *Excuses and Lies for All Occasions*, you'll find help for the workplace, friendships and dating, family and other loved ones, your own inner thoughts, and infractions such as unpaid bills. Finally, because famous people lie more than the average prevaricator, we present you with a jaw-dropping panoply of excuses and lies from the filthiest of the filthy.

Though the words contained in this book will help you with lying panache, the execution is still up to you. To amplify the many tips sprinkled among these pages, following are a few basic principles to keep in mind. Add details to your lie; the more realism you lend, the more believable your story. Make sure your lies reflect your personality; some of the lines in this book might not be quite "you," but it's possible to rephrase slightly to add your own flair. Don't stumble over your words; be prepared beforehand so that you can fluently narrate your fallacious tale. Add half-truths or even whole truths into your lies so that the two become indistinguishable and one adds veracity to the other; before long, you won't even know the difference. Finally, keep track of your lies. Liars are most frequently caught because they tell two different stories at two different times, so memory is crucial.

From the most stuttering rationalizer to the baldest-faced fabricator, *Excuses and Lies* will not only provide the best falsehoods for the widest variety of situations, it will help those who still value honesty to shed that useless mantle and get with the human program. Whether or not you believe all this, of course, is up to you—for all you know, we could be lying.

The Workplace

WHEN YOU JUST CAN'T MANAGE IT

FOR SOME REASON, WHEN YOU GET a job, the expectation is that you will arrive on time and show up every day; overall, most managers assume that work will be your priority. That's understandable, because you probably lied to get hired in the first place. Studies show that most résumés are full of misrepresentations: 71 percent increase tenures of previous jobs, 64 percent exaggerate accomplishments, 60 percent overstate the size of departments managed, 52 percent cite partial degrees as full, and 48 percent inflate salary history.

No matter your stellar background, sometimes work will be incompatible with your personal needs, and that's where workplace excuses and lies come in. The day-to-day grind practically requires that you fudge the truth. Whether it's explaining your tardiness, coming up with an excuse for playing hooky, buying extra time for a deadline, blaming technology, or providing context for why you've fallen asleep on the job, this chapter will equip you with every line necessary.

Meeting your own needs serves a larger purpose. You can't perform with all the pressure of punctuality and due dates, five-day work-

Don't Work—Just Lie

weeks and missed sleep. Often, it's just plain prudent to take a three-day weekend. And a spontaneous afternoon off will probably refresh you so much that your productivity will skyrocket. When you get down to it, your tardiness and absenteeism are for the good of the team—but they don't have to know that.

 ∾

Studies show that one-quarter to one-third of all workers tell lies to explain their tardiness or absence. When dallying away from the office, solid excuses and lies are critical, as the same data showed that most managers would be likely to fire employees who were repeatedly late or absent without explanation. Fortunately, nearly three-quarters of employers polled indicated they generally believe the excuses their employees give.

TARDINESS

I'm okay now, but I actually threw up on the way over here.

~

I couldn't find my keys anywhere.

~

I couldn't find my phone anywhere. And I couldn't call it from another phone, because it was dead.

~

My phone fell in the toilet.

~

My cat got out and I chased her all over the neighborhood.

You should have seen the line at Starbucks, and you do *not* want me here without caffeine.

~

I got pulled over. The idiot cop took forever. Fortunately, I didn't get a ticket.

~

Some moron stopped short and I slammed on the brakes, spilling my coffee all over myself. Not only do I have painful burns in unmentionable places, I had to go home and change.

I wanted to wait until after the laxative kicked in.

It took an hour to get over my fear of success.

The toilet overflowed and I had to wait for the plumber.

Some Greenpeace canvassers came to the door and I could not get rid of them.

A dive-bombing bird kept me captive, a prisoner in my own home!

PLAYING HOOKY & WORKING AT HOME

I had another panic attack. Don't worry—it wasn't about work.

It's most contagious in the early stages, and I don't want to expose everyone at the office.

I checked a friend into rehab on my way to the office.

My kid is sick. And so is the babysitter.

Two words—
bad oysters.

My boyfriend is
having his first
root canal and I
need to nurse him
through the pain.

My vet said I had
to watch her all
day to make sure
she doesn't have
a bad reaction to
the medication.

My identity was
stolen and I'm
just completely
overwhelmed
trying to straighten
it all out.

My doctor said I
really shouldn't
drive to work
because of my back.

If I work from
home I'll have that
much more time to
devote to my job!

I'm so much more
productive when I
work from home.

Tip: Track Your Absences

My therapist said I
need to improve my
work-life balance.

Nothing short
of perfect will
do for you.

MISSED DEADLINE

Didn't we cancel
that project?

I have it on my
schedule for
next week.

I need an assistant to
help me keep track
of things like this.

My doctor says if
I don't slow down
at work, I could
develop an auto-
immune disorder.

While it may be tempting to utilize the complete arsenal of
excuses presented here, do exercise some caution when
skipping work. Keep track of your "sick" days so that you
don't overdo it. Days flanking holidays are scrutinized, so
don't take too many of those. Be careful about absences
that dovetail with publicly known interests of yours—for
example, if you are known to be an avid skier, don't call in
sick after a huge snowstorm.

Everybody else
failed to get
me what I
needed in time.

The schedule
was completely
unrealistic.

෨

Every time I
thought about
the project, it
stressed me out.

Do you want it
fast, or do you
want it right?

෨

HIGH-TECH

Didn't you get it?
I uploaded the whole
thing last night.

It's a moving
target, and I want
the information
to be as up-to-the-
minute as possible.

෨

Word crashed
and I lost two
hours of work!

෨

I did my best. That's
all you can ask.

The file you sent
was corrupted.

෨

෨

I delegated that!

Your email went into my spam folder.

My computer got that new Chinese virus going around.

Someone hacked the server and placed a root kit that caused a buffer overrun precipitating a failure of AFP. As a result, the server unmounted and, unfortunately, I hadn't saved my document.

My carpal tunnel / eye strain is really acting up.

Yes, I need to spend three hours a day scrolling through social media. It's called market research.

Really? It opens fine on my computer.

I'm not jobhunting on LinkedIn. I'm spreading the word about our awesome company!

I forgot to charge my electric car last night, so I'm stranded at home!

OFFICE NAPS

I just started intermittent fasting and it's totally messing with my blood sugar.

~

I find that a fifteen-minute power nap improves my productivity immeasurably.

~

My chiropractor told me to rest my neck periodically in order to avoid having to make a worker's comp claim.

~

By accident I took the nighttime medicine.

I was just meditating on how we can innovate our value proposition to strategically leverage our core competencies.

~

Some idiot made decaf.

~

Amen.

Truth Fascism

QUITTING

I'm going
to be an
influencer.

It's my goal
to have a dozen
careers by the
time I'm 50.

I'm going to be
a pot farmer.

I'm going to
live off-grid in
a sustainable
tiny house.

I'm going to
miss our Saturday-
morning meetings
and midnight
conference calls.

You will always be
the gold standard
of bosses.

Alexander Kuzmin, mayor of the Siberian town of Megion, has banned city workers from using certain excuses, including "I don't know," "It's not my job," "It's impossible," and "I'm having lunch." A framed list of all twenty-seven prohibited excuses hangs next to Kuzmin's office. Those who refuse to uphold the ban "will near the moment of their departure." Fortunately, in America excuse-making is an inalienable right.

This is the best
job I've ever had;
I know it'll be
downhill from here.

~

I've learned so much
from you that it's
time to start my
own business.

~

I believe you deserve
someone who's 100
percent committed.

~

Now you don't
have to fire me.

~

Now you don't
have to pay me
unemployment.

You knew I was a
Millennial when
you hired me.

FIRING

Don't think of it
as losing a job—
think of it as
regaining a life.

~

We don't look at it as
downsizing—we look
at it as rightsizing.

Out-
Teching
Your
Boss

You'd be better served by an employer who's passionate about your work.

❧

We're delighted to be able to offer you this career change opportunity.

❧

You know that side-hustle you've been working on? Now it can be your front-hustle!

❧

Don't feel bad—this is our fault. We should have never hired you in the first place.

You're overqualified.

The office offers countless technical resources that make it appear that you're hard at work—a necessity for the two hours a day the average employee spends on personal activities. Options include "boss" or "panic" buttons that, when clicked, immediately cover any recreational screens with fake spreadsheets; digital recordings of office noises to make you sound busy; or the telephone for pretend conversations, a tried but true standby.

Liked Ones

WHEN THE TRUTH WILL HURT

IN THE COURSE OF NORMAL SOCIAL interaction, honesty is overrated. Indeed, if the truth were consistently told, the result would be social anarchy—the end of friendships, correspondence, entertaining, cohabitation, and dating. Social lies are frequently euphemized as tact or diplomacy (another lie—because what are those but misrepresentations or lies of omission?). However you justify your necessary prevarication, this chapter will provide you with the verbal ammunition for just about any communal situation.

Perhaps most closely related to tact and diplomacy is the category known as white lies, those uttered to make someone feel good (or not bad)—refraining from calling a new haircut a chop job, for example. Gray lies dig a bit more into relationship dynamics you'd rather not broach, such as assuring a gossipy friend of your trust in her. Amidst our busy, transcontinental, multi-media lives, staying in touch has become a particular onus, for which an arsenal of excuses is essential. The modern lifestyle also requires that we limit the number of invitations we accept—and extend. Finally, dating and dating sex introduce a host of opportu-

Every-
body's
Doing
It

nities for excuses and lies—and undoubtedly this misrepresentation is reciprocal.

The first lie we tell in our social lives is "Fine"; the answer to "How are you?" Why stop there? Excuses and lies grease the skids of social interaction, and if your social life isn't greasy, you've got some work to do—and these are the lines to help.

~

University of Massachusetts psychologist Robert Feldman studied undergraduates to determine everyday lying frequency. He discovered that 60 percent of the subjects lied during a ten-minute conversation; indeed, they told an average of two to three lies per encounter. He also learned that motivations for lying split along gender lines: women tended to lie to make others feel good, while men lied to make themselves look better.

WHITE LIES

You made that all
by yourself? It looks
so professional!

There's only one
word for this—
interesting.

No one would
even notice.

I think it's the
best thing you've
ever written.

Your taste is
so eclectic!

Remember—
looks aren't
everything.

They look
totally real!

It's probably just
water weight.

The decor really
reflects your
personality.

That is *so* funny.

It's delicious!

That is so smart.

I'm so happy
for you!

I'm sure he's just
really busy.

≈

≈

You don't look
a day over
twenty-nine.

Nothing's wrong.

≈

If you were
always reliable,
how boring
would that be?

I didn't know it
was a secret!

≈

I know you'll
make the right
decision.

GRAY LIES

Thanks for being
so honest.

≈

She wasn't good
enough for you.

≈

I'd tell you if
I thought you
needed therapy.

≈

I really like your
husband.

GHOSTING

I really like
your wife.

It's been so crazy
at work and I just
haven't had a
single moment to
call you back. For
four months.

Of course I'm
not jealous.

You'll make a
great parent.

I wasn't ghosting
you. I've been
living off-grid.

I can always
count on you.

I've been on a
digital detox.

It was just a
misunderstanding.

Lying
Makes
the
Man.

I didn't mean
it. BFF!

My phone's been
acting so weird!
Your message never
came through.

The wedding
planning has just
completely taken
over my life.

As soon as I hit my
deadlines, we'll
have dinner.

There's just so
much TV to watch,
I don't get out
much anymore.

It's so great to hear
your voice! However,
I'm in the middle
of something.

It's a very busy
time of year
for me.

According to David Livingstone Smith, author of *Why We Lie*, all lies perform one of two necessary functions: they either enable us to fit into society or they advance self-preservation. Psychologist Robert Feldman discovered that teens who lie most convincingly tend to be the most popular. As Feldman states, lying is "a social skill." Probably because of their aptitude for non-verbal cues, Feldman also found that girls lie better than boys.

I got a new
phone and all
my contacts
were lost.

I don't have
anything to wear.

Let's meet up after
the holidays.

My significant
other is having a
total meltdown and
needs my help.

TURNING DOWN INVITATIONS

I'm going to be
sick that night.

Since being
diagnosed with
social anxiety,
I've had to cut
back on parties
and gatherings.

I'd love to, but I
have to work.

I have to wake up
early the next day.

I'm going to be
introverting
that night.

I fell down and
hurt myself.

I can't be around
people who are
drinking.

It's just my friends
with kids—you'd
be so bored.

The environment
is being destroyed,
and you expect
me to celebrate?

It's only family.

I'm not inviting
anyone from work.

I can't be around
people who
are eating.

I don't have
enough chairs.

UNVITATIONS

It's just an
intimate gathering.

It's more of a
religious ritual
than a party.

It's just my sober
friends—you'd
be so bored.

I invited your
ex instead.

It's more of a
meeting than
a party.

I cleaned the
toilet last time.

Party? What party?

I didn't think you
would mind.

It's in honor
of someone you
don't know.

I totally paid
that bill.

ROOMMATES

I'll pay you back
next week.

I have no
idea how
your shoes
got ruined.

I'm just
having a few
people over.

**Tip:
Texting
Off the
Phone**

He hasn't "moved in with us." He just sleeps over every night.

I don't know whose vomit that is.

GETTING OUT OF DATES

That beer was yours?

I'm gay.

We weren't having sex in the shower—we were trying to conserve water.

I'm straight.

I'm married.

If you have friends who are obnoxious enough to call vs. text, remember: just because you answered the phone doesn't mean you're available. With long-winded friends, never feel like you have to talk beyond your comfort zone. Simply hang up then send a text message such as "Phone crappy—TTYL". For more impact, shout, "Oh my God! I have to go!" then hang up. A few minutes later, text "Sorry. Everything's okay. TTYL." After that, a good old-fashioned game of phone-tag can keep you safe for weeks.

LIKED ONES

I'm so attracted
to you that it
scares me.

Political activism
keeps me too
busy to date.

ى

I'm in a committed
throuple.

I'm asexual.

ى

I'm celibate.

You're too good
for me.

CASUAL SEX

Okay, just a
quick drink.

ى

I have to wash
my hair.

ى

I'm sapiosexual.
HMU if you get
into Mensa.

**Rescue
Call**

ى

I don't date.

The divorce is
in the works.

I really think
this could go
somewhere.

✎

✎

I've never done
this before.

I'm not
looking for a
relationship.

✎

I'm not looking
for a hookup.

✎

I'll call you.

✎

✎

Wow, it's huge.

I'll text you.

Technology can save you from a bad date or a boring
dinner party. Various online services will call your phone at
a pre-arranged time with a rescue call. You don't even have
to think of what to say—the recorded voice will prompt you
to repeat scripted lines, resulting in a realistic impression
that your roommate is locked out, a relative has been taken
ill, or there's a babysitter emergency. If you happen to be
having a good time, just don't answer.

LIKED ONES

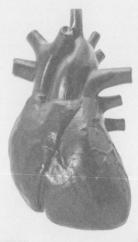

Loved Ones

WHEN YOU CARE
ENOUGH TO PREVARICATE

THOSE WHOM WE HOLD NEAR AND DEAR
will, from time to time, create the need for
clever lies and excuses. This doesn't mean
you love them any less—on the contrary,
you dissemble precisely because you love
them so much, whether to protect their feelings, preserve idealism, or guard against
painful truths. If you didn't lie, most likely
they'd eventually cease to love you.

Parents lie to their children for so many reasons. Perhaps a child isn't yet ready for induction into the mores of adulthood. Maybe a child deserves to have a myth remain intact. Finally, there isn't a parent alive who hasn't lied simply for expediency. Fortunately, these lies have a positive impact on children, as it aids them in becoming better liars, stimulating their imaginations and preparing them for the world. Of course, children turn right around and lie to their parents, and this chapter includes some sterling nuggets of filial deception.

It's between couples, however, that the richest opportunities for fabrication arise. If partners told one another everything in the daily struggle to stay together, the divorce rate would be higher than 0.38 per-

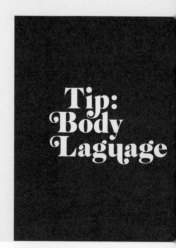

Tip:
Body
Laguage

cent per capita per year, and that's not even including serious relationships that haven't been ratified by official marriage.

The moral of this story? If you love someone, lie—and if you really love them, lie with scripted wit and creativity.

When delivering a lie—especially to the loved ones who know you best—avoid nonverbal "tells." Lying cues include forced smiles (real smiles involve the muscles around the eyes), formal phrasing (eschewing contractions such as "don't" and "can't"), pitch changes (non-lying vocal levels are relatively even), and erratic eye contact (truth tellers maintain contact, occasionally looking up and to the left, while liars look down and to the right).

TO CHILDREN

We're almost there.

~

It's not a kale
smoothie. It's
green ice cream!

~

It tastes just
like chicken.

~

Santa Claus
is coming!

~

The Tooth Fairy
just knows.

~

You can do
anything you want
if you really try.

He went to
doggy heaven.

~

This hurts me more
than it hurts you.

~

Mommy and Daddy
aren't arguing.
We're debating.

~

Daddy was just
giving mommy a
special backrub.

~

If you don't go
to college, you'll
end up driving
successful people
to the airport
for a living.

Yes, he's your
real father.

⁓

It's what's on the
inside that counts.

⁓

The best things
in life are free.

⁓

You can talk
to me about
anything.

⁓

It's perfectly normal.

⁓

You can't do
anything with a
liberal-arts degree.

If you have sex
before you're
married, you'll
go to hell.

⁓

Of course I
never smoked
weed / drank when
I was your age.

⁓

Of course I trust you.

TO PARENTS

I need more
unstructured,
child-driven
play time.

⁓

I didn't do it.

Someone made
me do it.

I learned it
from you.

~

~

My friend's mom
let *him* do it.

I didn't hear you.

~

~

Everybody's
doing it.

It's not my fault.
I'm just a child.

~

~

No one else's
parents ever
do that.

It's an *educational*
video game.

~

Dad said I
could do it.

**Born
Liars**

~

I don't feel well.

I misbehave
because you
work too much.

Nothing.

⁓

⁓

You didn't tell
me not to do it.

Nowhere.

⁓

Of course
grownups will
be there.

We're studying.

⁓

⁓

You can
trust me.

I don't know.

Humans begin lying shortly after birth. Six-month-old
babies get into the game through fake crying and laughing.
Two months later, they've added concealment and distrac-
tion. At two years old, toddlers bluff, and by their fourth
birthdays they've discovered the advantages of flattery.
Before they're ten, children will have learned to cover up
a lie—well in advance of their teenage years, when all that
prevarication will truly come in handy.

LOVED ONES

COUPLES: SEX

I had a hard
day at work.

Try me again in
the morning.

෴

෴

I have a headache.

My head says
yes but my UTI
says no.

෴

Maybe later.

෴

෴

It's not you. My new
medication has
sexual side effects.

I was in the
mood—yesterday.

෴

I ate too much
for dinner.

You look so hot
in those flannel
pajamas.

෴

෴

I'm way too
stressed about
everything
happening in
the news.

I need you to
pump me up for
my presentation
tomorrow.

CHEATING

It'll only take
a minute.

I have to work late.

ↄ

ↄ

Nobody can hear us.

I'm researching
online pornography
for an investigative
report.

ↄ

I just want to
express my
love for you.

ↄ

I'll get in bed in a
second—I just need
to shower first.

ↄ

If we don't do
it soon, we'll
forget how.

ↄ

Can you
believe my boss
scheduled another
business trip?

Size doesn't matter.

ↄ

ↄ

It's okay, honey.
We can just hold
each other.

I just look at dating
sites to remind
myself how lucky
I am to have you.

We were just
joking around
in those texts.

I'm not in the
least bit attracted
to them.

I created that
Tinder account
for my friend.

It just happened.

I was seduced!

We're just friends.

It was just an
innocent online
emotional affair.

I'm not in the least
bit attracted to him.

I'm not in the least
bit attracted to her.

Lying Hall of Fame

The lipstick on my
collar? My mother's!

I hate myself!

I've never been that drunk before.

It's not my fault, I have a sexual addiction.

I'm a child of divorce—what did you expect?

I wanted to buy a Porsche instead, but we can't afford it.

It didn't mean anything.

Everybody does it.

I'll never do it again.

Baron Munchausen, an eighteenth-century German raconteur, told such tall tales that they merited compilation in *The Adventures of Baron Munchausen*. His name was later immortalized in Munchausen syndrome, a psychopathology in which someone induces or fakes illness to gain sympathy and attention. And when caregivers, especially parents, inflict or project ailments onto those under their care, they're diagnosed with Munchausen syndrome by proxy.

LOVED ONES

BREAKUPS

You're too good
for me.

~

You're not happy—
and you deserve
to be happy.

~

I've decided I
don't believe in
monogamy.

~

We got together
for all the right
reasons, but we're
staying together for
all the wrong ones.

~

My therapist
told me we should
break up.

Your love has
made me
strong enough
to discover who I
am without you.

~

I think I might
be gay.

~

It's not fair
to you for
me to stay.

*Animal
Instinct*

I need to pursue
my dream of
becoming a
YouTube star who
travels the world
in a VW bus.

I remain
traumatized
by my parents'
divorce.

I think I might
be straight.

I'm a night
owl and you're a
morning person.

You're way out
of my league.

I hope we can
still be friends.

Your pets may not always be telling you the truth—lying
pervades the animal kingdom. Some frogs lower their
croaks to imitate larger frogs, thus attracting more females.
Mother birds have been known to feign broken wings to
divert predatory attention away from the nest. In one of the
most overt displays of cross-species lying, Koko, a sign-
language-speaking gorilla, tore the sink off the wall of her
pen and then, referring to her pet kitten, signed "Cat did it."

LOVED ONES

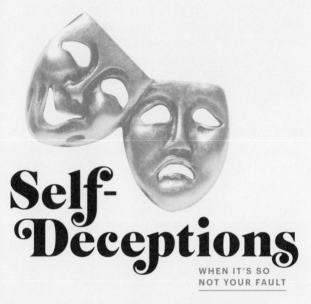

Self-Deceptions

WHEN IT'S SO
NOT YOUR FAULT

DESPITE ALL THE ADVANCES MADE IN THE
therapeutic industry in the twenty-first
century, with its devout advocacy of self-
awareness, inner-honesty is overrated. If
you really believed that you'd never exercise,
save money, achieve enlightenment, or kick
your vices, you'd be so bogged down with guilt
and self-loathing that it would be impossible to get out of bed in the morning. People
who lie to themselves are more confident and

self-assured than those who grapple with the truth of their own inadequacies. For true mental health, it's imperative to self-deceive; scientific studies actually support this.

While there are many ways to trick yourself into believing your own nonsense, the most fruitful and universally applicable is reliance on the concept of tomorrow: the metaphorical tomorrow, meaning not now. Tomorrow frees you of responsibilities and allows you to do whatever it is you want to do, guilt-free, whether you crave food, sleep, cigarettes, or shoes. You can start, quit, save, repent, contribute, or follow your dreams—tomorrow. Tomorrow is, in fact, the self-liar's best friend.

Tip:
Fake It
'Til You
Make It

If tomorrow were the only weapon in the arsenal of self-deception, however, this chapter would not be such a wealth of witty absolution, useful whether you're one of the few unhappy souls who never lie to themselves or, like most of us, you could just stand to brush up on your self-deception techniques.

Whether it's "I'll quit tomorrow" or "I deserve those shoes," spurious thoughts may help you achieve success. Books like *The Secret* recycle the concept of positive thinking, dubbing it the "law of attraction" or "intentionality"—if you think it, it will come—and there's some neurological data to back that up. Further, studies have shown that happy people are less honest with themselves than depressives, just one more reason to self-deceive.

GETTING FIT

I'm way too busy to start anything right now.

I'm going through a rough time.

I don't fit into my exercise clothes.

Studies show that dark chocolate is good for you.

I'll work out extra hard tomorrow.

Studies show that red wine is good for you.

Having treats is part of my self-care practice.

If I could afford a personal chef and trainer like Beyoncé, I'd be in great shape, too.

I honor my body's hunger cues. Right now my body is hungry for pizza, chocolate, and whiskey.

I feel like I'm coming down with something.

It might rain.

It's fat-free!

It's low-glycemic!

It's vegan!

It's organic!

I don't want
to irritate my
knees / IT band /
shin splints.

I'm out of sunscreen.

I'm doing
intermittent
fasting, so it's
fine if I eat this
chocolate cake
for dinner.

It's too hot.

It's too cold.

A pint is a single
serving.

I'm just retaining
water.

I'll start tomorrow.

SELF-DECEPTIONS

VICES

I'll quit smoking when I have kids.

~

I'm just a social smoker—I never buy a pack.

~

If I quit, I'll get fat.

~

First I'll switch to vaping, then chewing tobacco, then gum, then the patch. Then I'll quit.

~

I'm not addicted.

~

It's not illegal.

Weed is much better for you than tobacco.

~

Weed is much better for you than alcohol.

~

It's strictly medicinal.

~

It shouldn't be illegal.

Tomorrow...
It'll
Be
Good

I have a prescription.

I'm just a social drinker.

YOLO.

I don't drink before noon.

Red wine prevents heart attacks, but you have to drink it every day.

It's noon somewhere.

I need to drink—my job is really stressful.

It's not drinking alone if you have the TV on.

If you wait long enough, your vices may turn into virtues, allowing you to funnel your excuses and lies into other areas. In 2006, coffee was touted for raising mood and reducing disease risk; one medical review claimed "the more you drink, the better." In 2007, headlines celebrated the health benefits of red wine and chocolate, and now it appears that overweight people may live longer. Could cigarettes be far behind?

SELF-DECEPTIONS

It's not drinking alone if your dog is there.

It was on sale.

I'll stop tomorrow.

I had a coupon and it was on sale.

I'll stop after this political era.

If I didn't spend $50, I wouldn't get free the shipping!

OVER-SPENDING

I can always return it.

Buying tons of crap is good for the economy.

I was drunk when I bought it.

I just got my tax refund.

I had a coupon.

It will only appreciate in value.

They offered me interest-free financing.

It's an early birthday present. For me.

It's better to have bad credit than no credit!

I won't buy anything new for a year.

I'm just charging everything to build up my credit.

It's not binge-shopping. It's retail therapy.

I'll stop going out to dinner and buying lattes and I'll bring my lunch every day.

You've got to spend money to make money.

RELIGION & SPIRITUALITY

It's actually cheaper if you buy more than one.

I never said I was flawless— just forgiven.

I know God says "Love thy neighbor," but he hasn't met my neighbor.

~

Because I'm morally and spiritually superior, I have the right to judge others.

~

He's not a great moral leader, but even an imperfect vessel can do the Lord's work.

~

I wasn't unfaithful. My soul had an unresolved karmic debt with that hot yoga instructor.

My marriages always fail because I was born with a natal retrograde Mars.

~

I have no latent homosexual feelings whatsoever.

~

God made me as I am, and God doesn't make mistakes.

Pledge Allegiance

ETHICS

We give to the needy—all our old clothes.

I'm not looking through texts on her phone for no reason—I'm worried about her.

I shouldn't have lied, but my chakra cords are carrying negative ancestral heritage.

I'm not just snooping through his stuff—he could be in danger.

My spirit guides wanted me to steal that money.

You have to break a few eggs to make an omelette.

Shopping is good for the economy, which was brought into relief after the September 11th terrorist attacks. President George W. Bush told the country to "Get down to Disney World . . . and enjoy life, the way we want it to be enjoyed." British Prime Minister Tony Blair exhorted the world "to shop" to thwart recession. And then-Mayor Rudy Giuliani called New Yorkers "the best shoppers in the world" and urged them to action. When it comes to spending, patriotism is still the best excuse.

SELF-DECEPTIONS

Everyone lies on
their résumé.

~

Everyone cheats
on their taxes.

~

Everyone cheats
on the SATs.

~

If I don't do it,
someone else will.

~

I'm not here to
make friends.

~

What they don't
know won't
hurt them.

I'm a product of
my environment.

~

It's a victimless
crime.

~

I'm just doing
my job.

~

Sometimes good
people do bad things.

**Liars
for
Hire**

It's a huge corporation—what's a few missing office supplies to them?

It was a momentary lapse in judgment.

The heart wants what it wants.

It's not a crime.

I didn't know it was a crime.

It's for the greater good.

It's a rigged system.

Mistakes were made.

When you need a complicated lie, hire a professional. For a fee, a Minnesota company will lie for you. They primarily serve job seekers, and will, according to their website, "assist you in obtaining the fictitious reference, the little white lie, or the alibi that you need." Gaps in your résumé, lack of references, fired from a job? Paladin Deception Services can provide recommendations and proof of a stronger job history, among other services. What could go wrong?

Adulting

WHEN REAL LIFE
DEMANDS DISHONESTY

IN THE UNITED STATES, YOU'RE INNOCENT
until proven guilty—by someone else. You
may know full well that you've bent the
rules, but if there's no tangible proof, you'll
want to come out swinging with excuses
and lies to suit the alleged infraction.

Especially in today's overloaded world,
we're bound to face all kinds of accusations.
Overcrowding leads to scads of regulations

designed to delimit our shrinking boundaries, while inducing frustration and hair-trigger tempers. Whether you've been busted for talking in a quiet zone, cutting in line, returning a gently used good, denying a pile of bills, or breaking the law, the most important thing to remember is that rules don't apply to you.

When delivering excuses and lies for your defense, put yourself into the mindset of the victim. Perhaps you were subject to forces beyond your control—weather, conspiracies, emergencies, or the need to get out of the grocery store really quickly despite your twenty-item basket. Individuals confronting you have no idea why you needed to do what you did—they only care about themselves.

Tip: Get the Story Straight

Whatever your tactic to evade your persecutors, your goal should always be to get out of it. Sometimes this requires a good defense, while in other scenarios, turning the tables and attacking will serve you best. And when you can't come out swinging, words are all you have—the words contained in this chapter.

୬

With any excuse or lie, memory is critical. Whether your lie is challenged at a later date or you're called upon to lie in order to cover up a previous lie (a phenomenon known as the ripple effect), nothing exposes the liar like incongruous stories. If your lie involves others, make sure that you synch up—but don't match, as one of the hallmarks of group lies is verbatim recitation. For frequent fibbers, lie journals might even come in handy.

HEALTHCARE

No, doctor, I don't
smoke, and only
rarely drink.

∾

No, doctor,
I've never had
unprotected sex.
In fact, I'm a virgin.

∾

Flu shots don't work.

∾

Doctors' offices
are full of germs.

∾

I haven't seen
the dentist in a
few years because
you never sent
me a reminder
postcard.

Flossing makes
my gums bleed.

∾

I don't believe in
routine checkups.
If it ain't broke,
you know?

∾

I don't need
therapy. I'm
perfectly happy
being miserable.

∾

Antidepressants are
for crazy people.

∾

I'm not depressed.
I'm just way smarter
than all these
happy idiots.

BILLS

I've been out of the country on a human-rights mission.

*

The check is in the mail!

*

Clearly, it's identity theft!

*

Oops, I forgot a zero.

*

I ended that service months ago.

*

That bill was really confusing.

Your website is really buggy and wouldn't let me pay my bill. I shouldn't be penalized for your tech problems.

*

Stress-related medical problems necessitated my taking disability leave, and were compounded by misdiagnosed learning disabilities, causing me to have no income. In short, I can't pay you.

CUTTING IN LINE

I think I accidentally left my car running!

This is an express lane? I didn't realize!

I asked some guy to hold my place in line. Where did he go?

I just took my medication and in a few minutes I won't be able to drive myself home.

Oh, I didn't think you were in line.

I think I'm going to throw up.

My five jars of peanut butter and three liters of diet soda really count as just two items.

MAKING RETURNS

I was drunk when I ordered it.

The delivery guy dropped it!

It didn't have tags when I got it.

It smelled like that when I opened it.

*

*

My grandma got it for me— 'nuff said.

My dog peed on it.

*

GETTING PULLED OVER

I used it for two years and it just didn't live up to my wear-and-tear expectations.

A really awful song came on the radio and I had to change it—fast.

In 1908, César Ritz, founder of the tony Ritz hotel chain, exclaimed, "Le client n'a jamais tort," or "The customer is never wrong." The department stores Marshall Field's and Selfridges transformed the phrase into "The customer is always right," blazing the trail for consumer power. If you don't have a ready excuse for a suspicious return, there's a fallback: *you* are always right, whether or not you are lying.

I think I just had
my first out-of-
body experience.

~

Isn't Long
Island Iced Tea
nonalcoholic?

~

A flying squirrel
totally dive-bombed
my windshield.

~

It all happened
in an instant
when I sneezed.

~

Just because
it's in my hand
doesn't mean
I inhaled.

There was a bee
in the car.

~

I was just
going with the
flow of traffic.

~

The tree came
out of nowhere.

~

I was being chased!

~

I have to poop
really bad.

~

I'm a big supporter
of the Police
Athletic League.

CELLPHONES

Everyone talks and drives and eats at the same time.

Excuse me, but this is a very important call.

❧

Everyone takes selfies while driving.

Sorry—it's the doctor calling with my test results.

❧

Everyone crosses the street without looking up from their phone.

Sorry I missed your call! I was in a dead zone.

❧

You don't really have to put your phone on airplane mode while the plane's taking off.

You're breaking up! I'll call you back next week.

❧

This movie sucks, anyway.

No, that wasn't the toilet flushing. A really loud bus just passed by.

ADULTING

ONLINE

Sorry I tagged you in that photo! I think you look great with your eyes half-closed!

I'm not humblebragging. Being successful and attractive is so hard.

Sorry I tagged you in that picture with the strippers. I thought your wife was cool with it.

If my perfectly styled relationship, vacations, and décor make others feel inferior, that's on them.

I wasn't cyber-stalking your ex. I was just curious about what kind of loser would break up with you.

I was hacked!

Added Emphasis

Everyone lies on their online dating profiles.

Just 'cause I
like all his sexy
selfies, doesn't
mean I like *him*.

I didn't block you.
Must've been a weird
glitch or something.

#soblessed

I'm not a narcissist.
I'm a selfie artist.

Everyone uses
FaceTune.

I woke up like this.

#sorrynotsorry

I hate drama.

When it's necessary to add credibility to your lie, it's easy
to amplify your statement with one of these phrases: "You
have my word on it." • "I swear on my mother's grave." • "I
swear on the life of my first-born child." • "I'm looking you
in the eye." • "Now, I'm going to tell you the truth." • "If you
don't believe me, you can have your money back." • "Look
at this face—would I lie to you?" • "Pinky swear."

FLAKING OUT

I had to stay in with my cat.

My therapist told me parties were toxic for me.

My neighbor got drunk and blocked me in.

My horoscope said I should take my time today.

Oh, I thought the party was *next* Saturday!

I didn't want to steal your thunder so I stayed home.

My dog ate a box of crayons and pooped in technicolor on the couch.

Tip: Take Action

I accidentally took too many Ambien.

A wasp flew in
the house.

My toilet backed
up and flooded
the bathroom.

❧

❧

My spouse had
diarrhea.

I'm having bad
cramps.

❧

❧

My kid refused to
put on pants.

I think my kitchen
is haunted.

❧

❧

I got locked out
of my car.

I've got a cold sore.

When you're caught in questionable circumstances, words
alone may not be enough to deter negative consequences.
To ensure your safety, you'll want an arsenal of behaviors to
support your story. With a sickness claim, pretend to gag or
sneeze. Validate a worst-day-of-your-life excuse with deep,
crushing sobs. Underscore "I'm scared" with uncontrolla-
ble shaking. As a last-ditch effort, peeing in your pants will
get you out of almost anything.

Famously Infamous

EVERYBODY WANTS TO BE FAMOUS THESE DAYS, whether via social media and reality TV or for actual accomplishments. If they can't be famous, they want to look, dress, and act the part—and what better way than through excuses and lies? It's comforting to know that it's not just the little guy making stuff up. Everyone does it, including—or perhaps especially—those at the top.

Where the previous chapters have provided verbiage for your daily usage, here we present a rogue's gallery of famous liars and their enablers. The business section yields insight into how these companies got so big in the first place—lies and excuses helped. Sports present front-row opportunities to use performance-enhancing drugs and to gamble—and then lie about it. Among entertainers, there's little more entertaining than watching someone spiral out of control—and then attempt to spin it. Political animals provide galling examples, mastering the art of spin and cover-ups. The criminals are a sorry bunch; even though they excused and lied their hearts out, they got caught, and some even got punished.

Liar, Liar
Pants on
Fire

The lesson to gather from all these big shots is never to give yourself away. If you do something wrong, lie—whether or not you are under oath. If all else fails, you can always plead insanity.

Pathological lying, AKA *pseudologia phantastica*, has long been viewed as a symptom of an underlying mental disorder. A coping mechanism from early childhood, pathological lying tends to be unplanned, impulsive, and goal oriented. Pathological liars often believe their own lies (and thus can pass polygraphs). It may be partly physiological: one study suggests that these liars' brains have 26 percent more white matter, which has been linked with lying ability.

BUSINESS

"There is no proof that cigarette smoking is one of the causes [of lung cancer]. We believe the products we make are not injurious to health." —Tobacco Industry Research Committee, January 4, 1954

"The third quarter is looking great." —Kenneth Lay, Enron chairman, just months before the company reported a $638 million third-quarter loss, September 2001

"Chromium in this form is a naturally occurring metal that is an essential ingredient in the human diet." —Pacific Gas & Electric flyer, reassuring residents of Hinkley, California, who were living in deadly polluted areas, 1988

"Frankly spoken, it was a technical problem. We made a default, we had a ... not the right interpretation of the American law." —Matthias Mueller, Volkswagen CEO, defending its tricks to fool U.S. emissions regulators (aka "Dieselgate"), 2016

"It's not like I ever considered myself a bad person. I made a horrible mistake and I'm sorry."
—Bernie Madoff, whose Ponzi scheme robbed billions from investors, 2014

"The idea that fake news on Facebook ...influenced the election in any way is a pretty crazy idea." —CEO Mark Zuckerberg, after Facebook shared 50 million users' data with Trump-aligned Cambridge Analytica, 2016

"This is what happens when you work to change things. First, they think you're crazy, then they fight you and then all of a sudden you change the world."
—Theranos CEO Elizabeth Holmes, after the *Wall St. Journal*'s first published expose of her scam biomed startup, 2016

CELEBRITY

"The restaurant business is just so stressful, so stressful."
—TV chef and restaurateur Paula Deen, defending an employee who called kitchen workers "monkeys," 2013

"I truly apologize as this is NOT MY FAULT... but I'm taking responsibility." —Rapper Ja Rule, cocreator of the notorious Fyre Festival, a fraudulent and disastrous "luxury" music fest, 2017

"I want to apologize emphatically to Miss Philippians and Miss Columbia. This was a terribly honest human mistake and I am so regretful." —Miss Universe pageant host Steve Harvey, apologizing by tweet after mistakenly crowning Miss Colombia the winner, instead of actual winner, Miss Philippines, 2015

"As warped as this sounds now, I honestly began to feel that maybe I would be a bad mother if I didn't do what Mr. Singer was suggesting." —Felicity Huffman, explaining her part in the college admissions bribery scandal, 2019

Truthiness

"I don't know anything about it. It would be ridiculous for me to make any kind of assumption one way or the other." —Actress and feminist activist Scarlett Johansson on choosing to work with director Woody Allen, whose daughter accused him of molestation, 2014

"With respect to any women who have made allegations on the record, Mr. Weinstein believes that all of these relationships were consensual." — Sallie Hofmeister, spokeswoman for accused sexual predator and film producer Harvey Weinstein, 2017

Truthiness, Merriam-Webster's 2006 Word of the Year, is defined as "truth that comes from the gut, not books." The term was popularized when its creator, comedian and television host Stephen Colbert, satirized politicians who eschew intellectual reasoning when making important decisions. Use truthiness in your own repertoire of lying techniques: simply go by the truth that feels right rather than bothering with facts or empirical evidence.

"[I was] starving because I had not ate all day and possibly speeding a little bit ... and I wanted to have an In-N-Out burger ... [I'd had] one margarita at the event." —Paris Hilton, on why she got popped for drunk driving, 2006

"It was 2 in the morning and I was ambien tweeting." —Roseanne Barr, apologizing for the racist tweet that caused ABC to cancel her TV show, 2018

SPORTS

"After having two hip surgeries, I just wanted to get back on the field and give the Yankees their money's worth. It was my responsibility ... to get out there and play." —Baseball star Alex Rodriguez, who was suspended for doping, 2017

"It's very innocent. But I think the fault on my uncle was he just—he didn't have that bone in his body to look at it the other way. His naivete was his downfall in a way." —Michael Jackson's nephew Taj Jackson, on his uncle sharing his bed with children, 2019

"The origin of the Prohibited Substance must have been contaminated meat." —Cyclist Alberto Contador, after losing a Tour de France title for doping, 2012

"I'm sorry you don't believe in miracles." —Lance Armstrong in his 2005 Tour de France victory speech; he would later be stripped of his seven Tour titles for doping

"It was her birthday. The lady deserved a treat." —Sprinter Dennis Mitchell, who blamed his high testosterone levels on having sex with his wife four separate times the night before a drug test, 1998

POLITICS

"I have a disease, but I have no excuses. I'm an addict." —Former New York congressman Anthony Weiner, when sentenced to 21 months in prison for sexting with a 15-year-old, 2017

"I did not have sexual relations with that woman, Miss Lewinsky." —Bill Clinton, denying allegations of infidelity in the White House, 1998

"This was the largest audience to ever witness an inauguration, period."—Sean Spicer, on Donald Trump's sparsely attended inauguration, 2017

"Truth isn't truth." —Lawyer Rudy Giuliani, on why President Trump could be "trapped" into perjury by Special Counsel Robert Mueller, 2018

Our press secretary gave alternative facts to that." —Kellyanne Conway, defending Spicer's crowd-size lies, 2017

"I'm not a crook." —Richard Nixon, denying any involvement in the Watergate scandal, 1973

The Well-Planned Hoax

"That was locker room talk." —Donald Trump, on leaked tapes of him bragging about sexually assaulting women, 2016

"The United States plans no military intervention in Cuba." —John F. Kennedy, while planning the Bay of Pigs invasion, 1961

"I never held myself out as being anything other than human." —Elliott Spitzer, after exposure in a sordid prostitution scandal, 2009

"Read my lips: no new taxes." —George H. W. Bush, 1988

Successful hoaxes require skillful planning and execution, whether a brilliant forgery, a book-length lie, a fake anthropological find, or a false headline (such as the 1957 British news report on that year's bumper spaghetti harvest—from trees). The best of the best? Orson Welles's 1938 *The War of the Worlds,* a phony news broadcast about aliens landing on Earth that prompted unprecedented terror in the radio-listening audience.

"I liked beer. I still like beer." —Supreme Court Justice Brett Kavanaugh during his confirmation hearings before Congress, denying accusations of drunken sexual assault, 2018

OTHER CRIMINALS

"The voice on those tapes could be anybody." —Lawyer Jeffrey Lichtman, defending notorious Mexican drug lord Joaquin "El Chapo" Guzman, who was wiretapped by the FBI, 2019

"A very small part of my job was from time to time to find adult professional massage therapists for Jeffrey. As far as I'm concerned, everyone who came to his house was an adult professional." — Ghislaine Maxwell, purported "madam" to sexual predator Jeffrey Epstein, 2016

Supersize It

"His life will never be the one that he dreamed about and worked so hard to achieve. That is a steep price to pay for 20 minutes of action." —Dan Turner, father of Stanford University student Brock Turner, who was convicted of assault with intent to rape, 2016

"God, I hope she is found alive." —Scott Peterson, months before being convicted of killing his wife, 2003

"I did not have anything to do with these murders. Ever." —O. J. Simpson, ten years after the murders of Nicole Brown and Ron Goldman, 2004

The many compelling reasons to become famous include the chance to tell a "big lie," an intentional distortion of the truth for public propaganda. Most prevaricators only work one-on-one, but with the big lie, millions can be deceived. No lesser liar than Adolf Hitler stated, "In the big lie there is always a certain force of credibility . . . [people] would not believe that others could have the impudence to distort the truth so infamously."